Original title:
Brassy Tonics Under the Dragon Peel

Author: Kätriin Kaldaru
ISBN HARDBACK: 978-1-80562-568-1
ISBN PAPERBACK: 978-1-80564-089-9

Tales From the Smoldering Cauldron

In shadows deep, the cauldron swells,
With secrets brewed and ancient spells.
A flick of wand, a whisper soft,
From potion's depths, strange spirits loft.

The potion glimmers, green and gold,
A tale of courage, waiting to unfold.
With every drop, a story spins,
Of trials faced and strength within.

In smoky haze, the memories dance,
Of heroes brave who took a chance.
Each bubble bursts, a fable told,
Of daring deeds and hearts of gold.

Through twilight hours, the cauldron gleams,
Awakening all forgotten dreams.
With every stir, old legends rise,
Beneath the stars, their spirits sigh.

So gather round, and lend your ear,
To tales of wizards, far and near.
For in this brew, adventure brews,
In every sip, a world anew.

When morning breaks and night departs,
Remember well these magic arts.
For in each tale, a spark remains,
In smoldering cauldrons, love sustains.

The Epitaph of Fiery Infusions

In shadows cast, the embers glow,
A whispered name from long ago.
Beneath the earth, the potions lie,
Their spirits soar, they never die.

A draught of fire, a dash of fate,
In bubbling cauldrons, love awaits.
In every brew, a heart's desire,
Eclipsing all with passion's fire.

With every sip, a turn of time,
In molten warmth, the dreamers climb.
A tapestry of lives entwined,
In swirling fog, their threads aligned.

Once lost, now found in magic's hand,
Their epithets like grains of sand.
Through fiery infusions, they shall rise,
From depths of sorrow, brave the skies.

When night descends, and shadows creep,
The potions hum, a secret keep.
In every heart, the echoes sing,
Of lives lived bold, and the hope they bring.

So honor those who dared to dream,
In cauldrons deep, where potions teem.
For in their tales, the flames still burn,
And from the ashes, we shall learn.

Serpent's Whisper and the Alchemist's Brew

In shadows deep, where secrets swirl,
The serpent speaks, with emerald pearl.
A potion brews, in cauldron's glow,
The alchemist's hand, steady and slow.

Whispers echo through ancient halls,
A flickering light, as darkness falls.
Mysteries cling like mist on the moor,
Unlocking realms of forgotten lore.

With every stir, a tale ignites,
Of fortune sought on moonlit nights.
A sip of fate, a drop of dreams,
Reality frays, or so it seems.

Through slender vials, visions gleam,
The snake's sly grin, a silken scheme.
In every drop, a world unfurls,
Tales of magic, of wondrous pearls.

So heed the call, of serpent's sway,
Mix joy and sorrow, in grand display.
For in the brew lies destiny's twist,
Embrace the magic, you cannot resist.

Gleaming Spirits of the Embered Fable

Beneath the stars, the night unveiled,
Spirits dance where legends hailed.
An ember's glow, a flicker's flight,
In whispered winds, they find their light.

Each tale borne from the ancient fire,
Igniting dreams, igniting desire.
Around the hearth, they gather close,
With tales of love, of longing most.

Through branches bare, the shadows weave,
Looming softly as hearts believe.
Fables wrapped in silken threads,
Where hope ignites and never dreads.

Gleaming sparks in twilight's haze,
Kindle the heart in mystic ways.
For every ember, a spirit flows,
Binding the past with what still grows.

So listen closely, when night is deep,
For in each story, memories seep.
Ember's warmth, a timeless guide,
In fables told, where dreams abide.

Chromatic Nectar in Starlit Haze

In gardens wild, where colors bloom,
Chromatic nectar fights the gloom.
Petals glisten in twilight's kiss,
Life's sweet essence, a fleeting bliss.

Beneath the moon, the flowers sigh,
Their hues ablaze against the sky.
Every drop a story spun,
Of laughter shared, of love begun.

In stillness found, where shadows play,
Nature's bounty holds sway.
Sip the nectar, rich and bright,
Taste the magic born of night.

With every sip, the spirit lifts,
Dancing light in blissful shifts.
In starlit haze, enchantments swirl,
Colors awaken, dreams unfurl.

So wander deep through blooming fields,
For every heart, this nectar yields.
In vibrant hues, let souls entwine,
In chromatic whispers, hearts align.

The Alchemy of Sunlit Shadows

In morning's glow, where shadows blend,
The sun's embrace begins to mend.
Each ray of light, a golden thread,
Weaving tales where silhouettes tread.

Through emerald leaves, the whispers sigh,
Secrets shared beneath the sky.
The alchemist's heart, a spark of grace,
Finding beauty in every place.

Sunlit shadows dance and twirl,
In their rhythm, the daylight swirls.
Transforming moments, pure and sweet,
Every heartbeat feels the heat.

As daylight wanes and twilight calls,
The magic breathes within the walls.
In this alchemy of light, we find,
The art of living, heart aligned.

So cherish all those fleeting hours,
As shadows bloom with evening flowers.
For in the sun and under skies,
Alchemy lives where love complies.

Alchemy of the Shimmering Brew

In cauldrons deep, the colors swirl,
A tapestry of fate begins to unfurl.
With whispered chants and secrets old,
Alchemy's magic, a sight to behold.

Dust of stars and a dragon's tear,
Mixed with moonlight, so crystal clear.
With every stir, the essence grows,
In shimmering brews, enchantment flows.

From herbs of the wild, the forest's breath,
To potions that dance with life and death.
In each concoction, a story hides,
The alchemist's heart, where magic abides.

Old tomes reveal their ancient ways,
A flickering light in shadowy bays.
Spells entwined with a wisp of fate,
In bubbling brews, we find our state.

Beneath the stars, let the potion rise,
With every blend, a spark in our eyes.
For in this art, the world we spin,
In alchemy's grasp, we find within.

Elixirs in the Moonlit Glade

Beneath the silver of the moon's embrace,
In glades where shadows softly lace.
Elixirs gleam in night's bright glow,
A dance of magic, a tale to sow.

Whispers of fairies on the breeze,
Nature's bounty, a heart to please.
Potions brewed with a delicate hand,
Secrets spilled on the soft, warm sand.

From petals plucked in the pale moonlight,
To dew-kissed dreams that take their flight.
Every sip, a journey anew,
Elixirs of wonder, cloaked in dew.

In twilight's hush, mysteries unveil,
With every drop, the stories sail.
In moonlit glades, adventures gleam,
As we sip from fate's enchanted dream.

Rest by the stream, let the essence flow,
In nature's arms, feel the magic grow.
For under stars, the world feels right,
Elixirs shine in the peaceful night.

Reverberations of Lava Streams

Deep in the heart of the fiery land,
Where earth and fire join hand in hand.
Lava streams dance in a molten glow,
Reverberations of power flow.

With rumbling roars, the mountains speak,
A symphony of earth, both fierce and meek.
In trails of ash, stories are woven,
The pulse of the planet, endlessly proven.

Each bubbling brook, a tale to tell,
Of creation's forge and eternal swell.
Heat and heart in a timeless scheme,
In the reverberations, we chase the dream.

From molten core to skyward blaze,
The dance of nature, in wild displays.
Through the smoldering paths, spirits rise,
In the echoing roar, wisdom lies.

Nightfall drapes in a cloak of fire,
As stars awaken, fueling desire.
With every pulse of the earth's own drum,
In lava streams, we find where we're from.

Sips of the Celestial Dragon

High above in the twilight sky,
The celestial dragon takes to fly.
With scales of gold that shimmer bright,
It brews elixirs in the depth of night.

From clouds spun soft like cotton candy,
Each drop a wish, every sip dandy.
With laughter that echoes among the stars,
A taste of dreams, from Jupiter to Mars.

In crystal chalice, stardust swirls,
A tapestry of fate unfurls.
Sips of magic, woven with grace,
In dragon's breath, we find our place.

Let the world below seep away,
As we drink in light with a grand array.
Celestial wonders, we hold them dear,
With sips of the dragon, we conquer fear.

So raise your cup to the endless skies,
To dreams painted bright where starlight lies.
In every sip, the universe gleams,
A celestial dragon, the custodian of dreams.

Revelations in the Hearth's Glow

In the warmth where shadows dance,
Secrets whisper, chance to glance,
Crumbling embers, tales unfold,
Of ancient myths and treasures bold.

Flickering lights, a guiding spark,
Illuminating paths through dark,
Hearts entwined in love's embrace,
Finding home in ancient grace.

Echoes of laughter fill the air,
Magic weaves a silent prayer,
As stories linger, nights grow long,
In hearth's glow, we all belong.

With every spark, a dream ignites,
Stirring hopes like starry nights,
Here we gather, wise and true,
In the warmth, our spirits grew.

Beneath the mantle, still and bright,
Lies a world of pure delight,
In harmony, we share our lore,
Revelations forevermore.

Sizzling Currents of Stardust

Across the sky, the cosmos twirls,
In whispers soft, the stardust swirls,
Each grain a wish, a fleeting dream,
Sizzling currents like a stream.

In twilight's kiss, the magic roams,
Through galaxies, we find our homes,
The universe pulses, alive with sound,
In the dance of fate, we are bound.

Every shimmering spark ignites,
A tapestry of endless nights,
With every heartbeat, starlight flows,
In depths of silence, wonder grows.

Cosmic rivers beckon and call,
Drawing us gently through it all,
Each radiant moment, a path we seek,
In the vastness, we find our peak.

So let your spirit take to flight,
Through the galaxy's embrace so bright,
In sizzling currents, our souls unite,
Together we shine, a brilliant light.

The Riptide of Alchemical Dreams

In bubbling pots, where secrets brew,
Alchemists toil, both wise and true,
They weave together earth and sky,
Transforming worlds with every sigh.

Riptides swirl in mystic streams,
Guiding hearts through wildest dreams,
With every drop, a story's cast,
In the depths, our souls are vast.

Elixirs made from starlit dew,
Awakening senses, fresh and new,
In potion's blend, our fates entwine,
Alchemy's art is divine.

From whispered spells, the shadows rise,
Illusions dance before our eyes,
In every mixture, possibility gleams,
We sail upon alchemical dreams.

So seek the path where potions flow,
In the riptide, allow love to grow,
For in the magic of the night,
We find our hearts take sacred flight.

Potions from the Heart of Flame

From fire's heart, the potions flow,
Brewing magic, a radiant glow,
In cauldrons deep, dreams come alive,
Pouring forth, our spirits thrive.

Ginger and sage, with a pinch of salt,
Creating wonders, so none can fault,
In every breath, the warmth surrounds,
As joy awakens in riddle sounds.

A dash of hope, a sprinkle of grace,
In the cauldron, find your place,
For every remedy, a tale remains,
Echoing softly through joys and pains.

Laughter kindles in every mix,
Unveiling life's most tender tricks,
As potions weave through air so sweet,
Binding hearts where lovers meet.

So gather 'round the fire's embrace,
Share the wisdom, find your space,
In potions brewed from flames aglow,
We'll pour our hearts and let love flow.

Misty Fables of Golden Nectar

In twilight's glow where shadows play,
The whispers weave through the misted day,
Golden nectar in a fragile cup,
Dreams of slumber gently rise up.

Fairy lights dance on the forest floor,
With tales of old, they softly implore,
To sip the honey from nature's hive,
And feel the magic come alive.

The brook hums low 'neath a crescent moon,
Each droplet sings a timeless tune,
Enchanting echoes, softly spread,
Guide wandering hearts where few have tread.

A fable woven with threads of gold,
Of whispered secrets and laughter bold,
In the cool embrace of dew-kissed leaves,
Nature's bounty is all that it gives.

So heed the call of the twilight breeze,
Let your spirit roam with joyous ease,
For in this realm where dreams collide,
The misty fables with you abide.

The Fables in Glistening Botanicals

In gardens lush where secrets bloom,
Glistening woods dispel the gloom,
Petals whisper to the softest air,
Fables dance in a realm so rare.

With colors bright like a painter's dream,
Each blossom holds a magic theme,
Tales of wonder, in colors told,
In botanicals, the fables unfold.

Fragrant wonders drift on by,
Carried forth on the breeze's sigh,
With each drop of rain that falls anew,
Life's tapestry weaves, in every hue.

In the moonlit glade, shadows intertwine,
Glistening leaves with a soft divine,
Nature's essence, both wild and free,
In botanical wonders, we find our glee.

From bud to bloom, the stories go,
In every seed that dares to grow,
The glistening fables of earth's embrace,
Paint a picture of time and space.

Wind's Whisper of Potent Essence

Upon the breeze, a secret sigh,
Wind carries tales from the sky,
Whispers of herbs, ancient and wise,
Essences dancing, a sweet surprise.

Through fields of lavender and thyme,
Nature's bounty in perfect rhyme,
The potent lore of the earth weaves tight,
In the heart of night, it ignites the light.

Each breeze a messenger, prompts the air,
With scents that twirl, inviting care,
The laughter of leaves, a verdant delight,
In every gust, dreams take flight.

A cauldron brewing with fragrant grace,
Wind's essence can time and space,
With every breath, life's potion swirls,
Whispered secrets, both grand and pearls.

So let the winds guide your heart's quest,
In every essence, find your rest,
For in the gusts of the morning sun,
Nature's stories are never done.

The Brewmaster's Hidden Vault

In caverns deep where shadows hide,
The Brewmaster's magic does abide,
With bubbling cauldrons, potions bright,
In hidden vaults, they dance with light.

Measured drops of ancient lore,
Crafted with care, forever more,
Elixirs steeped in dreams and time,
A symphony, brewed to the perfect rhyme.

Mossy stones and twisted roots,
Whispers float from forgotten suits,
The alchemy of joy and strife,
In each concoction, there's a life.

From fragrant herbs to fruits of vine,
Each drop, a story—potent, divine,
The Brewmaster's hands, deft as the wind,
With every sip, a journey begins.

So venture forth with a trusting heart,
In the vault where eternal arts,
The brew awaits, an invitation clear,
For hidden treasures bring us near.

Melodies Stirred in Molten Vessels

In cauldrons deep, the shadows play,
Whispers of magic, night turns to day.
Each bubble bursts a tale untold,
In liquid dusk, their secrets unfold.

With flickering flames, the notes arise,
A symphony born beneath ancient skies.
Echoes of dreams in heated embrace,
Dancing like starlight, a spectral grace.

Crimson and cobalt, a painter's delight,
Swirling rhythms, igniting the night.
As potions shimmer, so spirits soar,
In this alchemy, hearts start to roar.

From copper tongues, a chorus sings,
Of journeys through realms on ethereal wings.
Melodies weave like threads of gold,
In molten vessels, their stories unfold.

Tapestry of Forgotten Elixirs

Woven together, each hue and taste,
A tapestry rich, that time can't erase.
Elixirs forgotten, in shadows reside,
Whispered in dreams, where secrets abide.

Glimmers of hope in bottles align,
Curiosities dance, a dance so divine.
Each potion a rune, a spell of the past,
In memories' weave, their legacies cast.

With touches of twilight, this fabric of fate,
Reveals hidden truths, while visions await.
The colors entwined, like whispers of air,
In this magical web, none are aware.

From violets deep to the amber hue,
Every thread sings of the heart so true.
A balm for the weary, a cure for the sick,
In forgotten elixirs, enchantments stick.

Underneath the Embered Canopy

Beneath the boughs where embers glimmer,
The world holds its breath, shadows shimmer.
In fiery whispers, the night speaks loud,
Starlit dances, wrapped in a cloud.

Crickets weave songs of soft lament,
While fireflies spark in a flickering rent.
Underneath this canopy, hearts intertwine,
In the warmth of the glow, romance does shine.

Secrets linger as the night unfolds,
With stories of youth, that time gently molds.
Magic resides in this embered flight,
Where love's gentle cadence ignites the night.

In the hush of the dusk, all worries cease,
Wrapped in enchantment, hearts find their peace.
With every sigh, the whispers do bloom,
Underneath the canopy, hope breaks the gloom.

The Weaving of Fiery Tongues

In the hearth's glow, where flames align,
The weaver spins tales, both harsh and fine.
Fiery tongues whisper, with crackling grace,
Eager to share secrets of time and space.

Threads of passion ignite the night,
Each flicker, a tale of joy and fright.
In the dance of the flame, old legends arise,
Spun with a tremor, beneath watchful skies.

With each flick, a heartbeat ignites,
In the fiery tapestry, magic ignites.
Lessons of ages, with warmth imbued,
In shadows they blossom, in light they are viewed.

The weaver delights in the chaos embraced,
Crafting a world where dreams interlaced.
Fiery tongues sing of life's ardent song,
In the heart of the flame, we all belong.

Glistening Elixirs Beneath Scales

In the depths where the secrets hide,
Glistening elixirs, magic inside.
Beneath the scales, treasures of lore,
Whispering tales of the ocean's floor.

A flicker of light in the darkened well,
Where potions brew and enchantments swell.
Mysteries dance in the bubbling brew,
Tales of the lost, of the brave and the true.

Crystals sparkle, a kaleidoscope gleam,
Bottled wishes escape like a dream.
Each drop a promise, each swirl a chance,
Inviting the heart to a whimsical dance.

Awake in the night with a potion's embrace,
Time slips away in this enchanted space.
For beneath the scales lies a world of delight,
Glistening elixirs, alive in the night.

Potions of Gold in the Twilight

In twilight's embrace, where shadows play,
Potions of gold guide the lost stray.
With whispers of winds and moon's gentle sigh,
Dreams ignite softly, like stars in the sky.

A flick of the wrist and a shimmer of chance,
Crafting the magic, invoking the dance.
Cauldrons bubble with secrets untold,
Transforming the dusk into treasure of gold.

Each potion a journey, a tale to unfold,
Flavors of twilight in bottles of old.
Brewing with care, with a pinch of delight,
Eclipsing the shadows, igniting the night.

Hope drips like honey, sweet on the tongue,
In potions of gold where dreams are sprung.
Let the twilight linger, let the magic flow,
For within every sip lies the beauty of glow.

Elixir Dreams in Celestial Mist

Through celestial mist where the night breezes flow,
Elixir dreams blossom, the heart starts to glow.
Rippling light dances on waters of fate,
Crafting enchantments that shimmer and wait.

Stars twinkle softly, each one a delight,
Stirring the potion beneath velvet night.
A splash of stardust, a twirl of the sky,
Painting the dawn as the shadows drift by.

With whispers of wishes, the echoes of dawn,
Elixirs emerge, as the moonlight is drawn.
Suspended in time, as the galaxies spin,
Awakening dreams, let the magic begin.

Drawn to the night, let your spirit ascend,
In the celestial mist, may your heart comprehend.
Elixir dreams waiting, in bottles aglow,
Each sip a journey where magic can flow.

Cacophony of Colors in Night's Haven

In night's haven bright, where colors collide,
A cacophony sings, let the magic abide.
Swirling and twinkling, a vibrant parade,
As potions of wonder in shadows are made.

Emerald greens and the sapphire blues,
Dancing in rhythm, embracing the muse.
Each bottle a story, each hue a delight,
Inviting the dreamers to savor the night.

With laughter of fairies and whispers of trees,
A melody floats on the softest of breeze.
Colors entwined in a tapestry bold,
Cacophony of joy in the night to behold.

Chasing the laughter, drawn by the light,
A feast for the senses, in shadows of night.
Let the colors guide you, let your spirit soar,
In night's haven bright, find the magic in store.

Whispers of Metallic Elixirs

In twilight's embrace, where shadows play,
Glistening vials hold secrets at bay.
Golden liquid, a shimmer divine,
Reveals ancient tales in each precious line.

Night creatures stir, with a shimmer of scales,
Brewing enchantment, beyond earthly trails.
The clink of glass resonates with delight,
As whispers of magic awaken the night.

Flickering flames dance in silvery light,
Crafting the potion that warms like the night.
A flick of the wrist, a sprinkle of spice,
Transforms the mundane to marvelous twice.

In corners unseen, where dreams intertwine,
The heart of the elixir begins to shine.
Each drop a promise, a wish softly spoken,
Binding the magic, ensuring it's not broken.

So raise up your chalice, let spirits ascend,
For in each metallic glimmer, we mend.
In the realm of the magic, we find our true selves,
In the whispers of potions, our essence delves.

Secrets in the Scaled Boughs

High in the trees where the shadows entwine,
Lies a secret, a treasure that's truly divine.
With scales that shimmer like stars in the night,
The boughs hold wisdom, both ancient and bright.

Underneath foliage where whispers reside,
The scaled creatures gather, a mystical tide.
Their eyes like lanterns, aglow in the dark,
Guarding the secrets of each hidden lark.

Through branches twisted, a tapestry spun,
Tales of the whispers, of moonlight and sun.
The heartbeat of magic, a pulse in the air,
Invites all dreamers to sit and to share.

With each gentle rustle, a promise is found,
In melodies woven from nature's own sound.
The secrets of boughs, a song yet to sing,
Awaits every seeker who dares to take wing.

So wander, intrepid, through shadows and light,
Unlock all the wonders that dwell in the night.
For the world holds enchantments in every soft sigh,
In the secrets of scaled boughs where the echoes fly.

The Potion of Fiery Spirits

Within the cauldron, embers ignite,
A fiery potion comes to life in the night.
Crimson and gold swirl in passionate dance,
Calling the brave for a daring romance.

With herbs from the ground and whispers of flame,
The spirits awaken, eager to claim.
Each dash of the potion brightens the soul,
Energizing hearts, making the whole world whole.

A flick of the wand, a snap of the air,
The potion of spirits brings magic to bear.
In cups raised high, let laughter abound,
For fiery elixirs make worlds spin round.

In shadows where dragons and dreams intertwine,
The potion of spirits does more than define.
It invites the heart to soar and to leap,
Where magic flows thick, stirring souls from deep.

So come, take a sip, let the warmth weave through,
Transforming the ordinary into something new.
For in this concoction, the true magic lies,
In the potion of fiery spirits, everyone flies.

Echoes from the Wyrm's Nest

Deep in the mountains, where echoes collide,
Lies the lair of a wyrm, with treasures inside.
Glistening scales like the moonlit sea,
Guarding the echoes of what used to be.

Whispers of ages, forgotten and clear,
Are carried on winds, both ancient and near.
The heart of the mountain beats low and deep,
In dream-laden shadows, where secrets still sleep.

Firelight flickers, casting stories untold,
Of battles and glories, both daring and bold.
With each breath of wind, tales begin to flow,
From the maw of the wyrm, a mystical glow.

Adventurers gather, their courage aflame,
To seek out the wyrm, to call out its name.
For in every echo, a lesson awaits,
And the wisdom of ages unlocks ancient gates.

So venture, brave hearts, where the wild wyrm roams,
To uncover the echoes that lead you back home.
In the whispers of fire and stone, take your rest,
For magic lies waiting in the wyrm's ancient nest.

The Heartbeat of Tonic Realms

In the dusk where shadows play,
Whispers of the night do sway,
Beneath the stars, a secret sings,
The pulse of worlds in potion brings.

Drifting through the silver streams,
Liquid life in quiet dreams,
Each sip a tale of ancient lore,
Awakens magic evermore.

In glassy realms where spirits weave,
Captured hearts learn to believe,
With every heartbeat, time's own dance,
Tonic realms call forth a chance.

The world unfolds with gentle grace,
A hidden door, a sacred space,
And in the taste, a story's thread,
Where all who drink are gently led.

So raise your glass to fateful nights,
To all the wonders, joys, and lights,
For in each drop, a universe,
The heartbeat of our souls immerse.

Legends Carved in Ethereal Sips

Upon the breeze, an echo calls,
Of timeless tales in ancient halls,
Legends steeped in flavored zest,
Awake the dreamers in their quest.

A potion brewed from twilight skies,
With every drink, the past replies,
Each sip a journey through the years,
Where laughter mingles with our tears.

Beneath the moon's soft, silver gaze,
We find the truth in twilight's haze,
A dance of flavors, rich and bold,
In every cup, a story told.

With every drop, the stories weave,
Of heroes brave who dared believe,
In realms where friendship knows no end,
Legends arise, we shall ascend.

So raise a toast to yesteryears,
To dreams ignited, hopes and fears,
For in each sip, a spark ignites,
Our spirits soar to wondrous heights.

The Melodious Hatch of Mystic Brews

In cauldrons deep, the magic brews,
A symphony of vibrant hues,
With every stir, a note ascends,
The melody of life it sends.

Through misty veils, the whispers greet,
A dance of flavors, pure and sweet,
Each sip a chord, a vibrant phrase,
That lingers long and deeply plays.

In crystal cups where dreams unite,
The world awakens to delight,
Each swallow crafted with a care,
The bump of joy through time and air.

Beneath the stars, the secrets twine,
In mystic brews, our spirits shine,
With laughter ringing through the air,
The hatch of magic everywhere.

So let us share this wondrous gift,
In every brew, our hearts will lift,
Together bound in harmonies,
The world transformed, our spirits free.

Elysian Mists of Transcendent Flavors

In twilight's mist, the flavors roam,
Elysian realms, a liquid home,
Each sip a kiss of cosmic light,
Transcendent dreams take graceful flight.

Between the sips, the universe breathes,
A tapestry of tangled leaves,
Flavors dance, a sacred art,
Awakening the dreaming heart.

In every glass, the stars aligned,
A journey through the grand designed,
With hints of magic woven through,
The essence of the rare and true.

So raise your chalice, let it shine,
In every drop, the worlds entwine,
The elysian mists, a soft embrace,
In every sip, a joyful trace.

Together, lost in fragrant dreams,
Through shadowed paths and silver beams,
With every taste, we feel it bloom,
Transcendent flavors chase the gloom.

Sun-kissed Draughts of Dragon's Breath

Upon the hills where sunlight flows,
A potion brews where magic glows.
With golden warmth and whispers light,
It dances wild, a soaring flight.

Each drop, a spark of dragon's pride,
In every sip, adventures ride.
The heart ignites, the spirit swells,
In sun-kissed draughts, enchantment dwells.

With fireglass chalice, dreams take wing,
Of ancient tales and winds that sing.
Beneath the sky, where shadows play,
The dragon's breath will light the way.

In forest glens where creatures roam,
The heart of magic finds its home.
With every taste, a story spun,
A journey shared, two souls as one.

As twilight falls, horizons blend,
The draught draws close, it claims a friend.
In whispered vows, the night reveals,
The thrill of life, the truth that heals.

Harmonies Beneath the Scaled Canopy

In emerald depths where shadows weave,
The songs of creatures, hearts believe.
Each leaf a note, each branch a rhyme,
In whispers soft, transcending time.

The scaled beasts twirl in graceful flight,
Beneath the stars, they spark the night.
Their harmony, a gentle breeze,
Invites the world to ebb and tease.

Embers flicker as stars align,
A rustic dance, a sip of wine.
The echoes linger, secrets shared,
In melodies, enchantments dared.

The moonlight bathes the forest floor,
As guardian spirits sing and soar.
In twilight's embrace, we find our tone,
Together lost, yet never alone.

With every chord, the heart takes flight,
In scaled canopies, pure delight.
A tapestry of dreams replete,
In nature's arms, our souls entreat.

Elements of Ecstasy in the Mystic Vale

In hidden groves where echoes play,
The elements weave a bright array.
A touch of earth, a wink of air,
In mystic vale, a moment rare.

With water's flow, the heart finds peace,
In every ripple, woes release.
From fire's spark, creation blooms,
In ecstasy, the spirit looms.

Around the stones where wisdom gleams,
The vale unveils our truest dreams.
With fervent hope, we chase the light,
Through verdant paths and starry night.

The whispering winds call out our name,
In vibrant echoes, hearts aflame.
An odyssey of joy unfolds,
In nature's lore, our fate beholds.

With every breath, the elements sing,
In unity, the world takes wing.
To dance in joy, to laugh, to weep,
In mystic vale, our promises keep.

Luminous Libations of the East

In twilight's glow where shadows gleam,
The lanterns flicker, softly beam.
A potion brewed of star-dust dreams,
In nightly hush, the spirit beams.

With each libation, wisdom flows,
From ancient tales the heart bestows.
The essence pure, a treasure rare,
In eastward winds, we breathe the air.

As jasmine scents the evening breeze,
The wonders wake in gentle tease.
A taste of magic, rich and deep,
In luminous nights, our souls to keep.

Each sip recalls a world unknown,
With fervent hearts, we're never alone.
In celebration of the night,
The stars above take sheer delight.

So raise your glass, let laughter spill,
In vibrant joy, our spirits thrill.
For in the east, where dreams collide,
Luminous libations will abide.

The Scrolls of Golden Infusion

In dusty halls where shadows creep,
The scrolls of gold in silence keep,
Whispers of wonders, tales untold,
Of ancient brews and treasure bold.

With fingers brushed by ancient dust,
The secrets unfold in magic's trust,
A potion brewed in twilight's glow,
Promises of joy, a friend to know.

From goblets lifted high with cheer,
To dreams inspired, drawing near,
Each sip a journey through the ages,
A glimpse of wisdom from the sages.

So dare to taste the golden bliss,
In every drop, a chance to kiss,
The echoes of enchantment's flight,
In every scroll, the heart's delight.

With every word, the magic spills,
In bubbling cauldrons and ancient hills,
For seekers who yearn for fortune's thrill,
The scrolls of gold shall hearts fulfill.

Timeless Libations in Draconic Lore

In caverns deep where legends dwell,
Timeless drinks weave magic's spell,
A dragon's breath within the vine,
Elixirs bright, a taste divine.

Through emerald flames and sapphire skies,
The casks hold tales that never die,
With every sip, a whispered lore,
Of dragons fierce and battles moar.

From goblets forged in molten fire,
A blend of hopes, a heart's desire,
With every draught, the spirit soars,
Awakens dreams, forever yours.

The lore infused in every taste,
A journey long, no time to waste,
For in each drop, the past shall blend,
The lore of dragons, a timeless friend.

Raise high your glass and make a toast,
To ancient times, we cherish most,
In draconic lore, our spirits entwine,
With every libation, our souls align.

The Dragon's Kiss of Spirited Harmonies

Under the moonlight's gentle grace,
Spirited melodies take their place,
A dragon's kiss, a tune so sweet,
In every note, our hearts shall meet.

The whispering winds through ancient trees,
Carry the songs upon the breeze,
From distant lands through valleys wide,
The soothing hum, our hearts confide.

With every strum, the magic sways,
As starlit pathways light our ways,
In harmonies where dreams align,
The dragon's breath, a spark divine.

So gather 'round the crackling fire,
And let the music lift us higher,
In rhythms churned by hearts ablaze,
We dance beneath the moon's soft gaze.

In every note, adventures bloom,
Where love and courage banish gloom,
The dragon's kiss brings forth delight,
In spirited harmonies of night.

A Fable of Sparks and Brews

In taverns warm, with fires aglow,
A tale unfolds of sparks and flow,
Beneath the laughter, whispers spin,
Of ancient brews where all begin.

With every pint held high and proud,
Legends breathe within the crowd,
In frothy swirls of liquid gold,
The fable blooms as hearts unfold.

Through clinking glasses, stories shared,
Of daring quests and those who dared,
A brew that binds, a spark that flies,
In every sip, a bond that ties.

So raise a cheer to friends we find,
In every journey, hearts entwined,
For in this fable, truths arise,
In sparks and brews, the spirit flies.

With every brew, a saga's birth,
A tapestry of laughter's worth,
In taverns' glow, where journeys meet,
A fable of sparks and life is sweet.

Nimbus of Gilded Nectar

In twilight's grace, the shadows play,
While whispers of nectar drift and sway.
Gold-tipped clouds in soft embrace,
Map the dreams of a distant place.

The winds gather secrets, sweet and rare,
Beneath the moon's gentle, silver glare.
Each drop a marvel, a taste of light,
Spilling stories in the hush of night.

Among the blooms that color the dark,
Lives a magic, a flickering spark.
With every sip, the heart takes flight,
Serenading the dawn's first light.

Through branches woven with starlit threads,
The dance of the fairies, as nightlight spreads.
In this nimbus, where wishes grow,
A tapestry blooms in the afterglow.

So raise your chalice to the skies,
To the nectar born from enchanted sighs.
For in its essence, we find our song,
In gilded nectar, we all belong.

The Ferment of Eldritch Fire

In shadows deep where nightmares creep,
Brewed in stillness, secrets keep.
The cauldron bubbles, whispers dire,
A strange brew is the eldritch fire.

With charcoal shades and fiery hues,
It murmurs tales that one must choose.
A potion dark with a raven's caw,
Stirred by hands veiled in fate's raw.

A flicker dances, wild and free,
In each plume of smoke, a mystery.
The heart quickens, caught in its spin,
For the darkest magic lies within.

Mystic forces twist and twine,
In every drop, a truth divine.
Hold your breath, let courage rise,
As flames entwine with ancient skies.

In twilight's air, the embers sigh,
A symphony heard when shadows fly.
The cauldron roars, a creature's breath,
In the ferment lies a dance with death.

Spirals of Luminous Harmony

In realms where light and shadow weave,
The dance of harmony begins to cleave.
Each spiral song a story told,
In whispers soft, both brave and bold.

Beneath the stars, the echoes bloom,
In every curve, a hint of gloom.
A tapestry spun from dreams so bright,
Guided gently by the moon's soft light.

With every turn, the earth will sigh,
As music swells to fill the sky.
Each note a vessel for hearts to find,
The luminous paths that fate has lined.

In gardens where the fireflies dart,
Harmony flows, a beating heart.
With open arms, we seek the grace,
Of spirals drawn in timeless space.

So gather close, feel the night's embrace,
In every spiral, a sacred place.
For within the light, as shadows roam,
Lies the promise of a kindred home.

The Cauldron's Roar at Dusk

As sun dips low, the mysteries churn,
In the cauldron's depth, old secrets burn.
Bubbles pop with an ancient flair,
A tale of twilight sings in the air.

With herbs and whispers, the moment swells,
In every potion, a story dwells.
The cauldron roars, a spell takes flight,
Unveiling wonders hidden from sight.

In the wrap of dusk, shadows dance,
Each spark ignites a daring chance.
With cauldron's song, the night unfolds,
Binding dreams in the hands it holds.

A world apart, where colors blend,
In each potion brewed, the paths extend.
The essence of twilight, dark and bright,
Awakens the magic of endless night.

So gather round, let the stories flow,
Where cauldron's roar sets the spirit aglow.
For in its warmth, we find our way,
Through dusk and dawn, night turns to day.

Visions from the Ember's Edge

In shadows cast by flickering light,
A whisper stirs the still of night.
Dreams are layered in glowing threads,
Enchantments linger where magic spreads.

Through the haze and ember's glow,
Secrets dance, elusive, slow.
Visions swirl in crimson lace,
Revealing truths we dare embrace.

Fires crackle; voices call,
A tapestry that weaves us all.
Bravely we chase what lies ahead,
In the warmth where shadows wed.

With every flicker, tales unfold,
Of bravery and hearts so bold.
Each ember holds a story clear,
Of dreams ignited, free from fear.

So heed the call of evening's tide,
Trust the hearth and let it guide.
For visions born from ember's edge,
Are treasures wrapped in fire's pledge.

The Alchemist's Lament in the Ashes

In alchemy where dreams decay,
The potions fade, the colors gray.
Once full of hope, now filled with dust,
What once was gold, now turns to rust.

A stirring heart, a fragile mind,
In twisted fates, truth intertwined.
We seek the spark, the missing piece,
In ashes cold, we yearn for peace.

Each vial shattered, echoes sound,
The alchemist's heart, forever bound.
To memories caught in fleeting grace,
In twilight's time, we lose our place.

With every swirl of potion's dread,
A whispered sigh, the life we've led.
For every experiment turned to night,
A hope remains, a flickering light.

Yet still we toil, through darkened days,
Our craft a dance, in myriad ways.
For in the ashes, wisdom grows,
An alchemist knows what fate bestows.

Recipes Written in Smoke

In cauldrons deep, where whispers rise,
A recipe cloaked in misty skies.
Stir the pot, let secrets blend,
As smoke reveals what dreams intend.

Pinch of stardust, dash of dreams,
Each ingredient flows in twilit streams.
With careful hands, we craft the art,
Of flavors drawn from the ancient heart.

From ember's kiss and twilight's song,
Each potion brewed where we belong.
A taste of magic, sweet and bold,
In every sip, a story told.

The air is thick with fragrant lore,
Inhaling wisdom, we crave for more.
For recipes whispered through the night,
Are meals of solace wed with light.

So gather 'round, both young and old,
As tales untold begin to unfold.
In every draught, enchantment flows,
As recipes written in smoke bestows.

Chasing Fireflies Through Brewed Reverie

In twilight's grasp, where shadows gleam,
We chase the glow, a fleeting dream.
Fireflies dance, a waltz of light,
Through brewed reverie of starry night.

With every laugh, a spark ignites,
In wonder's arms, we take to flight.
Each flicker draws us closer still,
To secrets hidden, hearts to fill.

We sip the potion, sweet and warm,
Finding comfort in the storm.
Shoulders brushed, hands intertwined,
In every glance, the stars aligned.

Through playful breezes, dreams ignite,
In summer's spell, we find our light.
Chasing splendor through the dark,
In every moment, a tender spark.

So wander forth, with spirits high,
In laughter's glow, let worries fly.
For life's a dance, a magical spree,
In chasing fireflies, we find the key.

Enchanted Sips from Mythic Lands

In the heart of the glade, where the fairies play,
A chalice of dew gleams in sun's gentle ray.
Whispers of laughter drift soft on the breeze,
As time slows to dance with the rustling leaves.

Elixirs of starlight poured into cups,
Bound by the stories our memory sup.
Each sip ignites magic, a spark in the soul,
Transporting our hearts to a realm beyond toll.

With every taste drawn from fountains of lore,
We're seekers of wonders, forever explore.
In shadows of twilight, dreams come alive,
As we drink from the dreams that help us survive.

The laughter of sprites, a tangible thread,
Weaves through the air as the day turns to red.
Held in our hands, a potion divine,
A journey awaits in each precious line.

So gather your friends, let the tales unfold,
For the sips of our myths are treasures of gold.
In enchanted embraces, let spirits renew,
For each drop is a promise of worlds yet to view.

Reflections in the Cauldron of Dreams

Glimmers of starlight dance on the rim,
As we peep in the cauldron, our hopes growing slim.
What futures are swirling in potion's warm haze?
Reflections of choices, a thousand pathways.

With smudges of ink, fate stirs the thick brew,
In the warmth of the night, our visions come true.
The whispers of ancients entwine with our hearts,
Guiding the way as the magic imparts.

Each drop of the elixir, a glimpse of the night,
Tales inked in the air, we bring into sight.
With friends by our side, shoulders gently sway,
In the cauldron of dreams, together we play.

What echoes of laughter and what tears once shed,
Are woven as threads in the potion we're fed.
The power of dreams, like a soft gentle stream,
Rising from depths where all wishes redeem.

So sip of the hope and embolden your mind,
For the cauldron of dreams holds the treasures we find.
In reflections of futures yet tenderly spun,
We weave our own stories, till the night's done.

Dawn's Nectar and Dusk's Ambrosia

In the blush of the dawn, when the world is aglow,
A nectar of visions begins its soft flow.
The whispers of morning wrap gently around,
As hopes take to flight, on the dew-kissed ground.

With every bright sip, a new promise is found,
Joy dances light-footed, in silence profound.
The sun breaks the stillness, where shadows once crept,
And the laughter of daybreak in our souls leapt.

As dusk wraps the sky in a cloak of deep blue,
Ambrosia rises, caressing the hue.
Fables of twilight weave softly like lace,
We gather the moments, sweet time to embrace.

With the nectar of dawn, a bright start unfolds,
Through dusk's gentle touch, our adventures are told.
In symphonic whispers, together we sing,
For each season's sip is a gift that we bring.

So raise up your chalice, let spirits imbibe,
In the circle of friends, let our dreams come alive.
For dawn's nectar and dusk's ambrosia shared,
Are treasures we hold, for our hearts have declared.

Golden Brews Under Celestial Wings

Beneath the vast sky where the stardust flows,
Golden brews flourish, as the wild magic grows.
Cradled in hands, warm as the sun's light,
The taste of adventure ignites in the night.

With every sweet sip, the worlds intertwine,
As the mysteries deepen, the cosmos align.
Celestial wings guide us through realms unknown,
In the hall of the heavens, we make our own throne.

The laughter of comets, the sighs of the moon,
Breathe life into brews, a celestial tune.
As galaxies whirl, we gather and share,
The golden ambrosia spun with tender care.

So clink your bright chalice with friends gathered near,
For the magic of moments is held ever dear.
Every flavor retold, like the stars shining bright,
As we sip on the stories that dance through the night.

With hearts full of wonder and spirits set free,
Golden brews under wings of the whimsical sea.
In the tapestry woven by fate and our dreams,
We savor the magic of life's flowing streams.

Harbinger of Fabled Brews

In cauldrons deep, the secrets steep,
A whisper stirs of magic's keep.
With herbs aglow and shadows blend,
The fabled brews, to souls they tend.

A pinch of starlight, a drop of dreams,
The potion brews in moonlit beams.
Each sip, a tale of old, retold,
Of heroes brave and treasures gold.

Through misty woods where spirits wail,
The liquid fire ignites the pale.
To sip the past, to taste the lore,
A journey vast through every pour.

The goblets clink, a ritual dance,
In goblin caves, they weave the chance.
To craft a brew that stirs the soul,
In every heart, their legend's goal.

So raise a cup, let magic flow,
The harbinger of tales aglow.
In every draught, let stories swirl,
A fabled brew for every world.

The Serpent's Sizzling Serenade

In shadows cast, the serpent glides,
A whispered tune where danger hides.
With scales that shimmer, secrets sing,
The sizzling serenade takes wing.

Underneath the ancient trees,
A melody dances on the breeze.
The sound entwines like lover's light,
A song that echoes through the night.

With every hiss, an enigma spun,
A tale of battles lost and won.
The serpent lurks, with eyes that gleam,
In twilight's glow, realities dream.

From mountain peaks to valleys low,
The snake enthralls where shadows flow.
Its music weaves a potent spell,
A warning bright, a whispered tell.

So listen close, for danger's near,
The serpent's song is steeped in fear.
Yet in its rhythm, wild and free,
A hint of truth lies deep, you see.

Interludes of Gilded Essence

In gilded threads, the stories bloom,
Interludes that pierce the gloom.
With laughter sweet, and sighs that speak,
The essence bright, the heart we seek.

A glimmer here, a shimmer there,
In every corner, a dream to share.
Through tapestry and colors bold,
The essence dances, tales unfold.

In fleeting moments, time suspends,
Where shadows meet, the daylight bends.
A sigh, a glance, hearts interlace,
In gilded hues, we find our place.

With every thread, the past we weave,
In whispered dreams, we dare believe.
Each essence glows with love and grace,
A circle formed, a warm embrace.

So cherish well these fleeting times,
In interludes, the magic climbs.
For in each spark, the best is shown,
The gilded essence, never alone.

The Siphon of Reverberating Legends

In echoes deep, the legends flow,
The siphon brews where dreams bestow.
With every tale, a voice revived,
In whispered strands, the tales survived.

Through centuries, the stories glide,
In shadowed corners, truths subside.
Each sip reveals a timeless spark,
A wisdom veiled within the dark.

With flowing grace, the legends pour,
From ancient tomes, to nevermore.
In every drop, a saga swirls,
The essence locked within our worlds.

So gather round, as fires burn,
Let every heart in yearning turn.
For in the siphon, magic bends,
And reverberates as time transcends.

In every echo, every tone,
The whispers linger, yet unknown.
So sip the legends, let them soar,
In endless night, forevermore.

The Enchantment of Aetherial Draughts

In twilight's glow, the potions brew,
With swirling mists of twilight hue.
A whisper soft, a gentle breeze,
Old magic stirs among the trees.

From crystal vials, the colors sing,
Of dreams and hopes that potion brings.
A taste of stars, a sip of night,
In every draught, a spark of light.

With careful hands, the witch allows,
The secrets shared by ancient vows.
For those who dare to sip the brew,
New worlds awaken, bright and true.

Each drop contains a tale untold,
Of battles fought and virtues bold.
In laughter's echo and silence deep,
The aether's blush inspires sleep.

The moonlight winks as shadows pass,
Mystical days made of glass.
In every glass, a wish is stirred,
A lucky chance, an echo heard.

Lizard's Legacy of Sultry Drinks

In sun-kissed dreams where lizards bask,
A recipe lost, a daring task.
With scaly skins and glittering eyes,
They craft the drinks that tempt the skies.

A cocktail sipped beneath the shade,
Where magic dances, unafraid.
With herbs and spice, a tincture rare,
A moment's bliss, a breath of air.

From ancient stones, the secrets flow,
Of lands where only courage goes.
With laughter cracked like brittle shells,
Their tales enchant like ringing bells.

The lizard's charm, a potion spun,
A legacy of warmth and fun.
In every drop, a history flows,
Of endless summers and moonlit glows.

So raise your glass to those who dare,
To bathe in sun and sing the air.
For every sip keeps fears at bay,
In lizard's legacy, we play.

Rhythms Found in Scorched Whispers

In night's embrace, where shadows creep,
A whispered tune, a secret deep.
The scorched remains of fires' glow,
In echoes soft, the rhythms flow.

A dance of embers, flickers bright,
With every gust, the tales take flight.
The winds carry what hearts confide,
In every note, dreams reside.

Through tangled woods, the music weaves,
A song of souls who once believed.
In every whisper, truths unfurl,
The serenade of dusk and pearl.

With hearts afire and spirits high,
The rhythms merge with the midnight sky.
For those who listen, magic sings,
In scorched whispers, hope still clings.

So gather near the glowing flame,
And in the darkness, call each name.
For every pulse, a heartbeat strums,
In rhythmic tales, the world becomes.

Synthesis of the Serpent's Breath

In silken threads of emerald hue,
The serpent's breath brings whispers true.
With ancient tongues of lore and fate,
A potion stirs that none can wait.

Through twisted paths where shadows play,
The essence hides, both wild and grey.
With every drop, enchantments swell,
The secrets locked in a bubbling shell.

In moonlit glades, their power glows,
A synthesis of highs and lows.
For every creature, wise and bold,
A tale is penned, a truth retold.

The breath of serpents, deep and wide,
With poison sweet and strength inside.
They weave a magic none can see,
In every heart, in every plea.

So gather round and sip with care,
For eons echo in the air.
In every glass, a world awaits,
The serpent's breath, the path it creates.

Crafter of Fabled Elixirs

In the heart of the forest, magic flows,
With whispers of secrets the ancients know.
A cauldron bubbles with dreams that ignite,
Creating elixirs that dance in the night.

With petals of starlight and dew from the dawn,
She gathers her herbs on the dew-kissed lawn.
A flick of her wand and the potion takes form,
Each sip a tempest, a storm to transform.

Vials of twilight and shadows entwined,
She brews in the moonlight, her craft so refined.
A careful concoction of hope and of grace,
In every drop, there's a glimpse of a place.

On shelves lined with wonders, her legends reside,
Each potion a tale where enchantments abide.
From sorrow to joy, every heart she can mend,
In her fabled elixirs, all spirits ascend.

So with each flutter of butterfly wings,
She conjures the magic that true alchemy brings.
In silence she works, as the faeries all cheer,
The crafter of fabled elixirs draws near.

Harmony in the Draconic Blend

Underneath the mountains, where shadows play,
A dragon of colors guards secrets at bay.
With scales of rich emerald and ruby so bright,
In harmony sings through the thick mist of night.

She brews in her lair, where the wild winds play,
A symphony woven in whiskers of gray.
With fire and ice, her ingredients dance,
In the heart of the blend lies a fateful chance.

Each potion a story, a balance so rare,
In the heart of the mix rests a tender care.
From the autumnal winds to the summer's warm glow,
Each drop a reminder of life's ebb and flow.

With wings that can whisk through a tempest's cruel tide,
The harmony sings, where the ancients abide.
In her molten embrace, both fierce and divine,
The draconic blend glimmers, forever entwined.

So gather, dear seeker, if courage you find,
Join the dance of the fire, be true and be kind.
In the heart of the dragon, in the warmth of her trove,
Discover the magic in each note that you wove.

Surging Waves of Golden Essence

Upon the shore where the mermaids sing,
Golden waves bring tales of the ocean's spring.
Mellow and sweet, like the sun's warm embrace,
Surging waves weave magic with delicate grace.

Jars filled with nectar, the color of sun,
Gathered by tides until day's race is run.
From seaweed and salt, to the soft moonlit glow,
The essence entraps all the secrets below.

In twilight's embrace, where the skies meet the sea,
Each drop of the essence sings wild and free.
In the cauldron, they swirl, like a dance in the night,
Beneath the stars twinkling with luminous light.

The taste of the ocean, a spark of delight,
Waves crash with a rhythm, a wondrous sight.
In the magical blend rests an age-old decree,
Surging waves carry whispers from the deep sea.

So listen, dear sailor, as the waves call your name,
Golden essence will guide you, igniting a flame.
With each gentle ripple, embrace what is near,
And let the waves of wonder wash away all fear.

Brews Beneath the Celestial Rim

Once a month when the stars dim the night,
Beneath the celestial, alight with pure delight.
A witch stirs her pot with a spoon carved from dreams,
Her brews catch the starlight, or so it seems.

Nebulas shine in the potion so bright,
Captured in vials, they shimmer at night.
With charms made of stories, both ancient and new,
She whispers the words of a magic so true.

Gathering shadows from crevices deep,
Her cauldron is filled with the echoes of sleep.
Elixirs that spiral like ribbons in space,
Brews beneath the rim, a transcendent embrace.

In the heart of her magic, the universe glows,
Each sip a journey, where wonder bestows.
To realms beyond reason, to dreams filled with whim,
The night unfolds wonders, beneath starlit brim.

So raise up your chalice to the heavens high,
Embrace the enchantments that twinkle and sigh.
For here lies the magic where the cosmos brightly spins,
In brews beneath the celestial rim.

Melodies of a Gilded Elixir

In glimmers bright, the potion swayed,
With honeyed notes, and mystic braid.
A whisper sweet, through shadows crept,
In dreams of gold, the secrets kept.

The chalice gleamed, a nightingale,
With each soft sip, the heart would sail.
To realms unknown, where wishes weave,
In gilded strands, the soul believes.

The laughter danced, like stars in flight,
Awake the spark, in velvet night.
With every drop, a tale unfolds,
Of love and loss, of dreams retold.

A tapestry of love entwined,
In every hue, a fate aligned.
A potion brewed, in twilight's glow,
In velvet cups, the magic flows.

So lift your glass, embrace the sound,
With gilded elixirs, joy is found.
In each sweet sip, let spirits rise,
For melodies weave through endless skies.

Secrets of the Celestial Cove

Beneath the waves, a treasure sleeps,
In whispers soft, the ocean keeps.
A cove adorned with shadows bright,
Where stars cascade in silver light.

The tide reveals, a cryptic song,
Of mermaids fair, where hearts belong.
In twilight's glow, the secrets dance,
A siren's call, a fleeting chance.

With every crest, a story wakes,
In swirling depths, the dreamer takes.
In salty air, the magic sways,
As moonlight winks through muted bays.

Lurking deep in cerulean blue,
The echoes of a love so true.
With every swell, the waters sigh,
In celestial whispers, dreams will fly.

So venture forth, with heart ablaze,
In hidden charms, find occan's gaze.
For secrets lost, the waves reclaim,
In cove's embrace, we play their game.

The Enigma of Spirited Melodies

In twilight's hush, the music calls,
A haunting note, as daylight falls.
With whispers soft, the shadows sing,
Of secrets spun on fairy's wing.

Among the trees, the echoes weave,
The sweetest sounds, they softly cleave.
A dance of light in silver rings,
Where every heartbeat, magic brings.

A lingering tune, like starlit grace,
In whispered dreams, we find our place.
With every chord, the spirit wakes,
In melodies, our soul it quakes.

So gather near, let voices blend,
In enigma's arms, our fears suspend.
For in the night, the echoes soar,
With spirited songs, we crave for more.

In timeless notes, we trust and find,
The enigma binds both heart and mind.
For every sound, a tale unfolds,
In spirited melodies, true magic holds.

Fiery Brews in the Night's Embrace

In bubbling cauldrons, secrets brew,
With sparks that dance in shadows new.
A crackling flame, a potion's spark,
In night's embrace, we venture dark.

The herbs entwined, their fragrance rise,
As starlit dreams twinkle in our eyes.
With every swig, the night expands,
In fiery leaps, we weave our strands.

A warmth that flows through every vein,
In laughter's light, we dance the plain.
With whispers low, the magic sways,
In fiery brews, we spend our days.

The night unfolds, a canvas bright,
With liquid gold in wondrous sight.
In every sip, a world unfurls,
As dreams take flight in vibrant swirls.

So raise your glass, embrace the spell,
In night's embrace, together dwell.
For every drop ignites the fire,
In fiery brews, we lift our choir.

The Charred Chronicles of Brewmasters

In the shadows where secrets play,
Brewmasters toil both night and day.
Hops and grains in a swirling dance,
Crafted potions, a bold romance.

With the flames that flicker and glow,
They summon spirits from realms below.
A touch of magic, a dash of spice,
In every barrel, the taste of nice.

Each kettle whispers tales of old,
Of adventures daring and tales bold.
The charred remains of well-worn dreams,
In every sip, a tale redeems.

The chestnut glint of amber brews,
In twilight's haze, the heart renews.
For those who wander and those who seek,
In every glass, the mystics speak.

So raise a toast to the artisans fair,
To the charred chronicles, magic laid bare.
In laughter and joy, let spirits soar,
For in their craft, we yearn for more.

Elusive Elixirs in the Abyss

Beneath the depths where shadows creep,
Elixirs dance in the water's sweep.
Mysteries brewed with the moon's soft hue,
Whispers of magic in every brew.

Bubbles rise like ethereal sighs,
Glimmers of dreams and forgotten cries.
In the abyss where the lost do roam,
Elusive potions lead us home.

A sip of solace, a draught of fear,
Secrets unfurl when the heart draws near.
With colors vibrant, as time suspends,
In this dark realm, where the light transcends.

Yet danger lurks in each swirling mist,
With every taste, a chance dismissed.
For elixirs brewed in the darkest night,
Can offer visions or dim the light.

So tread with care on this perilous path,
In the abyss, find both joy and wrath.
With chalice raised in the echoes' kiss,
Seek the elixirs, but do not dismiss.

Potent Mirages in the Dragon's Eye

Glimmers of gold in a dragon's gaze,
Potent mirages set the heart ablaze.
With each fierce glance, the world transforms,
In shimmering hues, creativity forms.

Legends spun in the flickering fire,
Visions take flight, our spirits conspire.
Enchantments woven with delicate thread,
In the dragon's eye, all doubts are shed.

The air is thick with magic's breath,
Dreams emerge from the shadows of death.
Chasing reflections in the flame's embrace,
Finding our truth in the dragon's face.

With each heartbeat, the dance ignites,
Potent spirits soar on daring flights.
For mirages hold more than mere deceit,
In their embrace, the brave find their seat.

So gaze with wonder, in the dragon's light,
For potent mirages come alive at night.
In each shimmer, a chance to embrace,
The magic that lingers in this sacred space.

Dances of Imbued Fire

In the hearth where embers gently glow,
Dances of fire put on a show.
With flames that leap and twirl in grace,
Imbued with magic, they carve their space.

Waltzing shadows in the dimming light,
Spirits entwined in the depth of night.
With each flare, a heartbeat is found,
In the rhythm of flames, the lost are unbound.

The air is vibrant with tales untold,
The warmth of memory, a touch of gold.
In flickers of passion, the stories ignite,
As dancers of fire embrace the night.

So let the flames guide our weary souls,
To the pulse of their dance, our spirit rolls.
In the embers' glow, we find our desire,
Forever enchanted by dances of fire.

With hearts alight in the night's embrace,
We join the flames in this timeless space.
For in every flicker, a tale does inspire,
A bond unbroken by dances of fire.

The Sweetness of Enigmatic Brews

In cauldrons deep where secrets stir,
A potion's hint, a thrilling blur.
With elderflower and mint entwined,
The essence of a dream confined.

A sprinkle of stardust, shimmering bright,
Weaving magic through the night.
Each sip a promise, a fable spun,
In every drop, the world is won.

Honeyed whispers from ancient trees,
Bring tales of love carried by a breeze.
When shadows dance 'neath silvered glow,
The brews invite, and hearts will flow.

Charmed by laughter and scents divine,
Gathering friends as stars align.
With every taste, the laughter swells,
Quenching thirst with secret spells.

For in each brew, a story waits,
An echo of truths, an ancient fate.
With every drop, the sweetness wakes,
An enigma that the moonlight makes.

Tonic Tales from the Serpent's Den

In shadows deep where serpents weave,
A tonic brews that few believe.
With scales of green and flickers bright,
Emerald depths in the heart of night.

Sipping stories from scaled lips,
Elixirs born from whispered grips.
A hint of danger with every taste,
Unveiling wonders, never a waste.

The flick of tongues and knowing eyes,
Revealing secrets, slumbering lies.
In dim-lit corners, legends blend,
Each draught a saga that won't end.

With phoenix feathers and dragon's tear,
Magic whispers that draw us near.
In every potion, a tale recast,
In the serpent's den, shadows are vast.

So gather 'round with hearts that yearn,
For every sip brings tales to burn.
In the warmth of potions, we'll find our way,
In the serpent's den, the night turns day.

Bright Brews in the Whispering Woods

In whispering woods where fireflies dance,
Bright brews await in a moonlit trance.
With berries sweet and laughter near,
The nightingale sings, inviting cheer.

A chalice raised to the starlit skies,
With every sip, the spirit flies.
Through ferny groves where magic plays,
The brews enchant in mysterious ways.

From roots of wisdom, knowledge sipped,
In every draught, the heart is gripped.
With nature's laughter in our souls,
United we dance, as the world unrolls.

The moon paints shadows on emerald leaves,
While golden brews gather the eves.
A potion mixed with laughter's glee,
In whispering woods, we are wild and free.

So linger long where the night unfolds,
With tales and brews the magic holds.
For in these woods, we weave our fate,
In wonderous brews, we celebrate.

Moonlit Spirits and the Dragon's Grasp

When moonlight bathes the world in grace,
And whispers linger in timeless space.
We gather 'round with spirits bold,
In dragon's grasp, new tales unfold.

With glimmers bright and laughter shared,
Each potion tells of how we dared.
A fiery brew that warms the heart,
In every sip, the boldest art.

Upon the winds, the echoes call,
As night unfolds, we stand enthralled.
In shimmering cups, our dreams ignite,
With every draught, we chase the night.

The dragon's breath, a fragrant kiss,
Unveiling wonders, pure bliss.
With tales of heroes and whispers fair,
We find our courage laid bare.

So raise your cup to the stars above,
In moonlit realms, we find our love.
For in the spirits, the magic grips,
As dragon's grasp adorns our lips.

Celestial Gastronomy of the Aether

In the realm where stardust gleams,
Feasts are laid on moonlit beams.
Each dish a whisper of the night,
Crafted by the cosmic light.

With silver spoons and crystal cups,
The heavens pour their magic ups.
Constellations spice the air,
Laughter rising, free from care.

From nebulous bowls, the flavors sing,
Of ethereal worlds where dreams take wing.
Galaxies swirl in a playful dance,
Inviting all to take a chance.

A banquet served on clouds above,
With each bite, a taste of love.
The stars, they twinkle in delight,
As taste buds soar into the night.

So gather 'round, let spirits soar,
In this celestial galley, forevermore.
For in this feast, the heart takes flight,
In the grand gastronomy of the night.

The Imprint of the Scaled Brew

In a cauldron deep and wide,
Bubbled brews the secrets hide.
Scaled and shimmering, darkly brewed,
A potion rich, a tale imbued.

From ancient tales the recipes flow,
With whispers of dragons in tow.
Each drop a legend, steeped in lore,
A drink that opens mystic doors.

With every sip, the past awakes,
Of winged beasts and whispered stakes.
The fire within ignites the night,
As shadows twist in flickering light.

In goblets carved from bone and wood,
The essence of magic understood.
A scale that glimmers, a tale to spin,
With every swirl, a world begins.

So raise your cups to the skies above,
To the imprint of magic and love.
For within the brew, a journey stirs,
Where the heart of adventure purrs.

Memories Encased in Smoking Dancers

In the haze of evening's glow,
Whispered secrets softly flow.
Dancers twirl with smoky trails,
Painting stories where time fails.

Each step a memory wrapped in smoke,
Of laughter shared and words bespoke.
A waltz of shadows, blurring fast,
In the twilight, echoes of the past.

Their movements cast a spell so bright,
Stars above, a gathering light.
With every spin, the night ignites,
A tapestry of spectral sights.

Through the mist, the echoes call,
Of dreams forgotten, great and small.
In the dance, a memory lends,
An embrace where time suspends.

So let the smoke and dancers twine,
Each pirouette, a sip of wine.
For in their grace, the past's entwined,
In the heart where dreams are lined.

A Ritual of Liqueur and Lore

By candlelight, the ancients gather,
In a circle where voices shatter.
With liqueurs rich, they weave a tale,
Of a world beyond the veil.

A sip of amber, a drop of gold,
In every glass, a story told.
The spirits rise, the laughter flows,
As the night unfolds its prose.

With each toast, the past is near,
In liquid magic, the heart draws near.
In the ritual, the seekers find,
The bond that ties all humankind.

So raise your glass to the skies above,
To tales of wonder, life, and love.
For through the liqueur, we share our fate,
In this dance of time, we celebrate.

With every swirl and clink of glass,
The moment lingers, never to pass.
The lore of ages in every toast,
In this enchantment, we all can boast.